BRIDGE
FOR
BLOOD

Illustrated by Ron Wing

BRIDGE
FOR
Blood

RAY YOUNG

 FOLLETT PUBLISHING COMPANY
Chicago   New York

By the Same Author:

BRIDGE FOR PEOPLE WHO DON'T KNOW
ONE CARD FROM ANOTHER

Library of Congress Catalog Card Number: 66-23812
Manufactured in the United States of America.
First printing

Design by Patrick J. Birch

Follett Publishing Company
1000 West Washington Boulevard
Chicago, Illinois 60607

T 0846

to Mike

CONTENTS

INTRODUCTION

There are more than thirty-five million bridge players in America today. Most of them are losers. When they play in duplicate tournaments, all they lose is status. When they play rubber bridge, they lose money.

This book won't help your status one smidgeon. It will help your bank account. It will convert you from a chronic loser to a consistent winner at rubber bridge. What you do at duplicate is not my concern. As a matter of fact, if you apply this book's basic principles to tournament play, you will undoubtedly take a bigger shellacking than ever.

I offer no apologies, because rubber bridge and

duplicate bridge are as different as Mutt and Jeff. And no one set of principles can make you a winner at both games. I know...from bitter personal experience.

This book is the result of one of the longest losing streaks an "unlucky cardholder" ever had. It took me five long years to smarten up. You'll find "every mistake in the book" in this book. I've made every mistake *once*. I've profited from my errors and so can you. You'll find here everything you need to know to stop being an "unlucky cardholder" (the flimsiest sort of self-deception) and start being a money winner. I guarantee it.

The Question

Is

"How Much?"

My losing streak started in Chicago one night in March, 1958. I had just moved from New York to Chicago as a migrant word-picker for an advertising agency. While I was living in a hotel, my family was back East trying desperately to unload a charming, prerevolutionary termite ranch in Westchester. People seemed unimpressed that the original mice had come over on the *Mayflower*. And I had a long wait before someone saw the beauty of undulating floors, hand-hewn but sagging beams, and a permanent, built-in play pool in the basement that flooded the furnace every time we had a particularly heavy dew.

I also had $350 of the hotel bookie's money

burning a hole in my pocket. A search through the Yellow Pages turned up, under "Bridge, contract," the address of a nearby card parlor.

Now, if ever there was a more willing sucker, it must have been the rube who bought the Brooklyn Bridge twice. Fresh from a couple of duplicate triumphs on Wednesday nights at the Pleasantville High School, I felt I couldn't go wrong, especially at such modest stakes as a quarter of a cent a point.

A kind lady graciously introduced me to the players. Ten hours later, now playing at two cents a point, my money had half vanished. Why?

5

Had I played badly? Heavenly days, no. Hadn't I pulled through that "unmakable" slam with a Vienna Coup? Had I bid badly? Mercy, no. Who else would have found that 800-point sacrifice against an almost certain slam? Had my partners been chowderheads? Not exactly, but why on earth had they refused to play my conventions? Why, indeed, had I, a good player, gone down to so bad a defeat?

If I tried now to catalogue my errors of that evening in this chapter, and I can look back even now with almost total recall, I could not do it, for it would run to three hundred pages. So you must be content with a short chapter and this cryptic answer: *In duplicate bridge, it's "how often" that counts. In rubber bridge, it's "how much" that counts.*

Memorize these words even before I explain them. These two sentences can save you a small fortune.

Now I will explain.

In duplicate the thoughtful player always asks himself, "How often will the rest of the players in the room arrive at this bid or make this play?" For instance, if he thinks most players will arrive at and make three notrump, he may prefer a riskier contract of four spades, figuring he will get a top for scoring the extra 20 points (three notrump equals 100; four spades equals 120). Sometimes he will even jeopardize a cold contract with a line of play that will land him an overtrick, if it is likely that the rest of the field will play it safe.

That kind of thinking is mental wrist-slashing at rubber bridge. Here the thoughtful player always looks at the price tag: "How much will it cost me if I stick my neck out?" "Is now the time for me to do it with the opponents vulnerable and us not?" "If I stretch to game to wipe out that partial, will my partner turn up with enough help to avert disaster?" "If I take that finesse, will it cost me a cold game?"

"How much?" That is the question I did not ask myself that evening. And that, in a nutshell, is why the bookie's money went down the drain.

I still can't bear to call it *my* money.

A
Few Price
Tags

My next few nights at the Chicago bridge parlor were equally disastrous. Hour after hour I watched my opponents rack up points by the thousands above the line. It is a tribute to my handicapping rather than to my bridge playing that I managed to survive.

Finally, after a particularly bad bloodbath, Ziggy, my luckiest opponent, offered to buy me "coffee-and" at an all-night hash house around the corner.

Ziggy was a droopy-lidded Austrian who had to be prodded into wakefulness each time his partner finished playing a hand. His catnaps as dummy seemed to have a marvelously refreshing effect on his play. For when Ziggy had to play a hand, he played it with gusto and an incessant machine-gun-like chatter of asides to the kibitzers. Once he had thoroughly inspected the dummy, he rarely paused in his play of the cards. But if an opponent paused, Ziggy would drum his fingers briskly on the table and comment to the kibitzers on the weather, the stock market, the sad state of the Chicago Cubs. All this jabber in an accent you couldn't cut with a cleaver.

Ziggy was awake and silent only after a partner had booted a hand. Since I had booted several, I was surprised at Ziggy's generous offer.

Over coffee, in an accent thickened with fatigue, Ziggy gave me my first lesson in rubber bridge.

"Look, Schnickellyfritz, I hope you have an oil well in your backyard. You bid and play like money was coming out from the ground. Maybe you got a money tree? Nein? O.K., Ziggy will tell you what's wrong.

"First rule. Don't play no more duplicate when you're playing for money. Rubber bridge is a game of partials. Duplicate no got partials. If duplicate had partials, Ziggy would win every tournament," said he modestly.

"How much is worth a partial?" he asked.

I allowed that a partial is worth 20, 30, 40, 60, 80, or 90 points.

"*Dummkopf!* A partial is worth 200, maybe 300 against good opponents. You don't bid enough to stop a partial. You don't bid enough when opponents have a partial. Two mistakes you make time after time.

"Next time you play with Ziggy, don't let opponents get first partial. Spend 200 points like down

10

one doubled vulnerable. Who knows? They might *not* double. Only costs you 100.

"If opponents do get first partial, then you got to kill it. Stretch your bid to game even if the odds are 8 to 5 against your making it. You understand odds, horseplayer? You bet on long shot when opponents have partial.

"When *you* have partial, you are big. Then you can make sacrifice. You can afford it. With 60 below line you can spend 500 points to stop game, 900 to stop slam. Without partial you can only spend 400 and 700.

"When you have game and partial and opponents don't have neither, you can spend 1100 points to stop slam. You like that, duplicate player? You like to sacrifice, but you don't know when to do it. Never—no, hardly ever—do it when opponents got game and you don't. The odds are 3 to 1 against your winning rubber. Give them their 700 rubber cheap.

"Well, old Ziggy's got to get up early and get back to the actuary business. Bridge lesson's over."

Take Ziggy's preachments to heart and you will save yourself hundreds of dollars throughout the years. Here they are for review:

> Fight like a tiger for the first partial. It's worth a minimum of 200 points.

If your opponents get the first partial, bid dubious games in an attempt to wipe out their advantage. A corollary is *don't* bid dubious slams in this situation.

The best time to sacrifice is when you lead by a game and a partial. The odds favor your winning the rubber.

The worst time to sacrifice is when your opponents are vulnerable and you are not. You're bucking 3 to 1 odds to win the rubber.

The
Short-Circuit
System

I wish I could say that Ziggy's lesson worked wonders with my game, but circumstances beyond my control intervened. My family arrived from the East and I was forced to give up my sessions at the bridge parlor.

My game actually deteriorated. I became hopelessly addicted to a system based on rigid point-count requirements. I wound up in a morass of weak bids and responses that flustered little old ladies and won nothing but fractional master points. I gained a drawerful of pink slips signed by tournament directors. I lost whatever common sense I'd had.

Fortunately, my rubber bridge was confined to

a few friends who also played the system. This home-style duplicate didn't hurt anybody. A big evening consisted of paying out a couple of dollars at two o'clock in the morning. Fun, but not very profitable.

Gradually the System lost its appeal. Some nights at regular duplicate sessions it would clobber the opposition. Other nights it wouldn't make a dent. Instead of restoring sanity to my game, the some-time nature of the System goaded me into devising a system of my own.

One night after getting deep into the wet goods before dinner at a neighbor's house, I concocted the following stew of conventional bids and dubbed it "the Short-Circuit System." It was designed as an anti-system system, because it almost guaranteed an opening bid every time, no matter what kind of garbage I might have picked up. By opening constantly, I figured I would deprive my opponents of the chance to make a systemic opening bid, thereby throwing a monkey wrench into their delicate bidding machinery. Here it is in all its artful idiocy.

The Short-Circuit System

OPENING BID OF ONE HEART OR ONE SPADE. A weak bid showing a four- or five-card suit and 10 to 12 points. A rebid of notrump indicates a four-card suit;

a rebid of the suit indicates a five-card holding. With equal length in both majors, open one heart to allow yourself an escape into one spade in case your right-hand opponent decides to convert his partner's take-out double into a penalty double.

Since the average bridge hand contains 10 points, you find yourself opening constantly, thereby depriving your left-hand opponent of the chance to make an opening weak two-bid, weak notrump, Neapolitan club, or what-have-you.

OPENING BID OF TWO HEARTS OR TWO SPADES. A "strong" weak two-bid with 13 to 15 points and a five-card suit or better.

The opportunity to make this bid occurs fairly frequently. Again it louses up your opponents' bidding gimmicks. And it has the additional merit of being a reasonably safe preempt—safer than the weak two-bids of 6-12 points now in vogue.

OPENING BID OF THREE HEARTS OR THREE SPADES. A strong bid showing 16 to 18 points and a five-card suit or better. With an average 10-point hand and three-card trump support, partner goes to game.

With only one bid and one raise, your opponents have little to go on in planning their defense. When you have 5–5 in the majors, you have a problem; but you have at least eight cards in trumps if you reach game in your first-bid suit, and you have a fighting chance to name your second suit if your partner responds with anything but a raise.

OPENING BID OF ONE CLUB OR ONE DIAMOND. A reasonably hefty short minor-suit opening of 15 to 17 points. It can show a long minor suit, which you can indicate by rebidding. With an average 10-point hand, partner can visualize game readily and either bid notrump (encouraging) or respond with one in a new suit (probing). Opener rebids one notrump to show a balanced hand and to deny a fit in whichever major suit the responder may have named.

OPENING BID OF TWO CLUBS. A "rockcrusher" of 20 points or more in high cards and distribution forcing to game. With an unbalanced hand, your first rebid shows your suit. With 24 high-card points or more and a balanced hand, make a jump rebid of three notrump. Partner can then assess slam possibilities with ease.

OPENING BID OF TWO DIAMONDS. A two-way bid showing either 18 to 20 points and a balanced hand *or* a solid long suit (not necessarily diamonds). Partner treads water with an automatic two-heart response until opener clarifies his holding.

If the opener rebids a suit, he shows a lopsided holding (A K Q x x x or A K J x x x x). Whereupon partner can gamble at three notrump, knowing that he has a good chance at six tricks in one suit; he can

16

raise the suit; or he can pass with a sigh of relief. The opponents can't get rich by doubling, and they may never reach an ice-cold game their way.

The reasons for this odd bid are fairly simple. A normal weak bid of two diamonds is woefully weak as a preempt. It immediately proclaims a poor hand from the roof tops and invites the opponents to enter the auction with a major suit. Also, in keeping with the "short-circuit" theory, the opportunities for opening two diamonds occur much more frequently when the bid has a double meaning.

OPENING BID OF TWO NOTRUMP. A weak bid showing at least ten cards in the minors and less than 14 points in high cards and distribution. This bid is nothing more than the "unusual" notrump put to work as an opening bid.

Partner must name his longest minor suit if he has a bad hand. With a long minor suit and a very bad hand, he should jump to four or five in his suit— the opponents must have game or even slam on ice.

With a reasonably good hand, responder can ignore the request for a minor and name a major suit, which forces the opening bidder for one round.

With an honor or two in one of the minors and stoppers in the majors, partner can take a stab at three notrump.

OPENING BID OF ONE NOTRUMP. A weak one notrump

indicating a balanced or semibalanced hand and 12 to 14 points. Partner responds with a Stayman two-club bid if he holds a four-card major or longer and 12 points or better. He can also respond with a pre-emptive jump to three in a minor or a simple two-over-one bid in a major—both bids indicating lop-sided distribution and less than 12 points.

Born of martinis, the "good ol' S.-C. System" seemed like the greatest thing since sliced bread by the time the brandy came round. We had to try it. So we did.

We rolled into the nearest duplicate session in the middle of the first board. No matter. There was

an opening. We hastily filled in a convention card, making sure to put down "occasional psyches" to cover our weak major-suit openings, and proceeded to play.

Maybe it was the gin and brandy fumes that befuddled the opposition. We chose to believe it was our beloved new gimmick. Even after booting three hands with abominable play, we came in second by a comfortable margin.

Obviously the millenium had arrived. We were ready to take on all comers at duplicate or rubber bridge. Of *course* it would work at rubber bridge. Why not?

Points,
Schmoints,
or Why the Systems Fail

Convinced that *veritas* had somehow emerged from *vino* and that the good old Short-Circuit System was unbeatable, we challenged two of the cockiest local experts we could find. A set game at a penny a point. Whoopee!

My partner had taken the precaution of checking the System out with *Probabilities in Contract Bridge* (Kibler, Telfer and Traub). According to the charts, we weren't about to stick our necks out.

Our weak one-heart and one-spade opening bids of 10 to 12 points were buttressed by the fact that partner's probable holding would exceed 8 points more than 50 per cent of the time.

Opening a four-card suit presented no problem. The charts showed clearly that partner would hold enough to dominate the opposition 65 per cent of the time—a comfortable edge, we thought.

Our other bids looked beautiful, too, downright fiendish as a matter of fact.

The game started with my partner and me licking our chops. The experts just sat there looking smug and reading our convention card with ill-concealed amusement. One of them allowed as how they played Stayman, but no "fancy stuff."

Four hours later, when the dust had settled, my partner and I paid up $85—apiece.

What happened? Well, I'll tell you.

Every time one of the lesser probabilities turned up, such as partner's holding a 3-point bust or a singleton in our suit, we got our brains beat out. Low-level penalty doubles cost us 500 or 800 points, and one innocent bid even cost us 1100 points.

To be sure, our opponents were required to back into the bidding with overcalls and takeout doubles. But they did so with aplomb and with devastating effect. Time after time an overcall in fourth position started them on their merry way toward bidding and making game. One takeout double led them to a successful slam contract with only 27 high-card points between them.

Once a losing psychology set in, we were constantly outbid in the duels for part scores. And when our worthy opponents stretched their bidding too far, it only cost them peanuts.

Sadder but wiser, I took stock of my beautiful point-count/probability system and threw it into the ash can. It had served a purpose, however. Here are a few of the things the debacle taught me.

There are "good" points and "bad" points. The horse sense to discern the difference can save you a fortune. For instance, contrast this hand ♠ K Q J x x x x ♡ A x x ◇ x x ♣ x which contains only 10 high-card points, with this hand ♠ x x ♡ K J x x x ◇ K J x ♣ A J x. Now you have 13 high-card points and a terrible hand. Your points are "bad" simply because they can't guarantee tricks.

One more comment on "bad" points: Singleton kings and doubleton queens must be sharply down-valued when the opponents enter the bidding. Knock a point or two off your count, and then if your total is too skinny, you can do one of two things: shut up or add a point for each card over four in your long suit. Good length is often an admirable substitute for poor strength.

It rarely pays to advertise weakness. Advertising a weakness at rubber bridge is an open invitation to have your throat cut. A conventional weak opening bid, especially in third position after partner has passed, proclaims that the power probably belongs to the opponents. Such an announcement encourages them to back into the auction and steal a partial. Even worse, it sometimes enables them to find a fit that can lead to a hard-to-bid game.

A corollary, at duplicate *or* rubber bridge, is that weak bids are often worth a trick to the opposition on offense or defense.

Probabilities are peachy only if you know when to apply them. Timing is everything in rubber bridge. There is a time to pull in your horns. There is a time to sacrifice. There is a time to stretch your bidding. If you play every hand in the limbo of pure probabilities, you had better have rich, doting relatives. Again we return to the two questions asked earlier: In duplicate bridge the question is "How often?" In rubber bridge the question is "How much?"

At duplicate, for instance, with ♠ A Q x x x ♡ A x x ♦ A x x x ♣ x and a bidding sequence of one spade, pass, two spades from partner, three hearts from the opposition, you park comfortably at three spades if the opponents let you buy the contract. There is every likelihood that you will bag an average board. To make game your partner, with a minimum response, would have to come up with the "right" cards, for example, ♠ K x x x ♡ x x ♦ K x x x ♣ x x x, and the probabilities are slightly against it.

With the above holding at rubber bridge, neither side vulnerable and your opponents having a 90 partial, you should ignore the probabilities and, having asked yourself "How much?" stretch for game. Foolhardy? Not at all. According to the bidding your partner has enough even with the "wrong" cards to hold your probable losses to down one doubled—a loss of 100 points and a terrible duplicate score. But looking at the bright side, in rubber bridge a successful stretch to game can save you a bundle of points. It wipes out the opponents' partial and with it any chance at a 700 rubber. Damn the probabilities—full speed ahead! The price is right.

24

The reverse of this rashness can also occur at rubber bridge. For instance, with opponents vulnerable with 60 on, you hold, as North, ♠ A Q J 10 ♡ K Q J x x x ◇ A K ♣ x. The bidding:

SOUTH	WEST	NORTH	EAST
Pass	Pass	2 ♡	Pass
2 NT	Pass	3 ♡	Pass
4 ♡	Pass	4 NT	Pass
5 ◇	Pass	?	

Knowing that your partner has one of the missing aces, do you push for *six*? All you need is a spade finesse to bring home your slam, and the probabilities give you a 50–50 chance. But you're a chowderhead if you take it. Look at the price tag. An ice-cold game in this case gives you 150 points below the line, saves you 200 points (the opponents can now only make a 500 rubber), and wipes out the threat of the opponent's partial (theoretical value, according to Swiss expert Jean Besse: 110 points). If you go down one, tack on another 50 points to what might have been, and your total loss comes to 510 points. Your slam, if successful, would net you 680 points (180 for the contract and 500 for the bonus). In short, you're betting 460 in the bank to gain 220 in the bush on a 50–50 chance. Do it with your money—not mine.

What these examples illustrate is that no system

can substitute for horse sense when you are playing for money. You must look at points and probabilities with all the suspicion of an auditor going over a horseplayer's books. You must constantly inspect the price tags. You must recognize that rubber bridge calls for a different kind of daring and a different kind of conservatism than duplicate bridge. Know the differences and you will know a healthier bank account.

The Gods
and the Odds
Favor the BOLD

The question "How much?" is usually frightening to the hacker. He is perfectly content to bid three spades and make four because "if the heart finesse hadn't worked, we'd never have made game, partner, and besides we're vulnerable."

On two counts the man is a mathematical moron.

Not vulnerable, bidding three spades and making four costs you 250 points (120 for your contract and an arbitrary 50 points for the partial against 120 for the contract and 300 for game). The potential loss "if the finesse hadn't worked" is only 190 points (50 for the set, 90 for the score, and 50 for the partial).

Vulnerable, the cost of conservatism goes up. Assuming the opponents are not vulnerable, you lose 650 points by not reaching for game with a 50–50 chance of making it (120 for the trick score and 50 for the partial against 120 and 700 for the rubber). The potential loss here is 240 (100 for the set, 90 for the trick score, and 50 for the partial). In short, the money odds are about 3½ to 1 in favor of stretching to game (820 to 240). Only a hopeless pigeon can ignore odds like these. The lesson is obvious: Don't pull in your horns just because you are vulnerable—lower them and *charge!*

"Aha!" says the hacker. "What if you get doubled?"

What if, indeed? The money odds are still slightly in your favor even if you go down two doubled (in the example above 640 potential loss against a potential profit of 820).

However, when your judgment tells you that you are making only a one-trick stretch to bid game, the opponents will rarely double. If they habitually double on the expectation of setting you one trick, please write me in care of my publisher. I want to cut into your game.

Of course, there is another delightful possibility when you stretch a little, especially when you do it calmly and confidently. The opponents may be goaded into a sacrifice, and then your dubious game can be converted into a money-in-the-bank double.

This possibility, plus the certainty of pure mathematics, leads Mr. Charles Goren to state flatly, "...you only have to make one doubtful game in three to come out with a profit." As usual, he is absolutely right.

What about stretching to slam? Does being bold pay off here, too? The answer is yes *and* no.

Pure mathematics indicates that you should always bid a small slam if given a 50–50 shot at it. A grand slam requires 2 to 1 odds in your favor.

Horse sense indicates that you should take stock

of the tactical situation before you plunge. Ask yourself, "Who is vulnerable and who is not?" "Who has a partial and who does not?" You will often find it pays to look for better odds.

Edward Mayer, author of *Money Bridge* and a player for blood from way back, states, "Slams are not the bread and butter but they are the jam of rubber bridge." When your opponents are vulnerable and you are not, go for the bread and butter. You need 2 to 1 odds in your favor to bid the slam (a 3–2 split in your outstanding trumps, for instance). For grand slam you need 3 to 1 odds in your favor at all times.

Does this mean you should turn from man to mouse in your slam bidding at rubber bridge? Not at all. When you are vulnerable and your opponents are not, you are odds-on favorites to win the rubber. You can afford to gamble on a slam that might depend on not one but two finesses. So you go down one and the opponents chalk up 100 points above the line (don't tell me they double slams). A small price to pay for a crack at a 750-point bonus, and you may have an even safer crack at it on the next deal. Another example of why it pays to *charge* when you are vulnerable.

In a nutshell, what this chapter is all about is something the experts agree on to a man: When in doubt, bid one more time. If this comes hard, try Geritol.

Part Scores...
And Why
They're Worth Fighting For

Occasionally it is my misfortune to cut as my partner a nice old gentleman who wears Brooks Brothers' finest shades of gray and at least a pound of starch in his collars. His backbone is singularly lacking in starch.

Time after time in competitive bidding situations he tosses in the towel without a fight. Invariably he explains his cowardice like this: "Well, partner, let them have the partial—we can't make game. We're off two aces, the king of clubs has to be sitting right, and you can't count on the diamonds splitting like that." (His post-mortems would make a coroner envious.)

That I knew full well we might not make game escapes him. That I was perfectly willing to bestow 100 points above the line on our opponents to prevent their gaining 60 points below the line strikes him as a senseless extravagance. But old dogs are old dogs, and I've learned the price of folly in preaching or teaching new tricks at the bridge table.

With my favorite partners I fight like hell to prevent our opponents' gaining a partial. They know, and I know, that a partial is always worth "invisible points" that mean the difference between profit and loss in the long run.

The experts are not agreed on how much more a partial at rubber bridge is worth than the arbitrary 50 points assigned to it at duplicate. In an attempt to answer the question, the Swiss expert Jean Besse studied one thousand part-score situations. He checked partials and partials converted to game and came up with the following results: *

Partial of 40 or More	Value
Nonvulnerable	90
Vulnerable (opponents not vulnerable)	110
Both sides vulnerable	220

John Crawford's rule of thumb is that it is worth 200 points to stop a part score, and he advocates

*Bridge World, December, 1964

bidding up to a point where you risk going down two not vulnerable and down one vulnerable. I'm with him.

I've found in practice that I am rarely hammered for a 300-point loss (down two doubled not vulnerable). The average price tag runs well under 200 points—perhaps because my opponents have been too "chicken" to risk doubling me into game, perhaps

because I've been able to crowd them one or even two tricks beyond their depth when they do take a bid away from me.

Partials should do more than just stiffen your backbone; they should have a marked effect on your bidding.

The existence of a partial militates against being locked into any system of rigid point-count requirements. For instance, if you have agreed to open one notrump on 16 to 18 points, you should forget the agreement if you have a partial of 40 or more. The preemptive value of an opening one notrump bid is such that you can afford to make it with as few as 12 points not vulnerable.

For example, with 60 on, you hold ♠ Q x ♡ x x x ◇ K Q J x x ♣ A x x. This hand, with most of its strength in the minors, offers only a flimsy defense against a heart or a spade contract. So why not conceal the five-card diamond suit and open one notrump? A number of good things can happen.

Your left-hand opponent, with more guts than brains, can overcall with a bad suit and get severely punished by your partner. He can sit there meekly and pass with a gold mine if he's the timid sort. About the worst that can happen is that you will be doubled, and then you can beat a hasty retreat to a prepared position—your diamond suit.

The upper limits of your opening one notrump bids should be stretched, too, especially in third position.

With 19 or 20 ratty points and even distribution, a short minor-suit opening of a club or a diamond issues an engraved invitation to your opponents to explore a profitable save with a major-suit fit if they can find one. By opening one notrump in first or second position, they may think twice about over-calling with a major at the two level. The danger of missing a slam is minimal with an intelligent partner. If he responds with two clubs, treat it as Stayman, and you still have an opportunity to explore for a slam.

In third position, if your partner has passed, you can safely forget about slam. If he passed with a decent major suit and 13 or 14 good points, accept your game and make a mental note not to have him as your partner again if you can possibly help it.

A good rule of thumb when you are considering an opening one notrump with more than enough points is to check your major-suit strength. With a poorly textured five-card suit, such as K J 7 6 2, you are better off bidding notrump. Even with a good four-card major, such as A K Q 10, you are better off bidding notrump. Because of the part-score situation your partner can easily be tempted to raise you with a worthless doubleton.

Other notrump bids should be stretched when you have a partial. Open two notrump with 21 to 24 points when you have 60 on. With less than 60 on, stretch the range and open two notrump with 20 to 24 points. Here again, you are preempting and sacrificing only a point or two in accuracy.

The opening three notrump bid is a waste of breath with a 20 or 30 partial. Open two of a suit and await developments. This gives your partner a chance either to announce a bust or to encourage a slam exploration.

A response of one notrump should be stretched most of all when you are trying to convert a partial to a game. Shade it down to four points and give your partner a fighting chance. With a ragged suit that your partner might leave you in, respond one notrump with as many as twelve points.

Your other notrump responses should not be stretched a smidgeon in my opinion. A two notrump response should mean 13 to 15 points. A three notrump response should mean 16 to 18 points. Opposite an opening bid these are safe responses and there is no need to sacrifice accuracy.

One good place to shade your point-count requirements because of a partial your way is when you are considering a strong opening two-bid. Sit up in your chair and bid it with one playing trick less than normal. This can have a magical effect on your partner. He knows at once that you did not open on garbage in hopes of converting the partial; accordingly, he will be less inclined to hide his strength under a basket. If he gets carried away, you can always calm him down with discouraging rebids. At least you encourage a probe for slam at a time when a partial could easily discourage it.

What about opening one-bids in a suit? When *you* have a partial, should you open light or strong? When your opponents have a partial, should you get into the bidding early with mediocre hands or sit back and sandbag with good ones?

Culbertson's answer was "Shade your bids downward if the opponents have a part-score and upward if you have the part-score." Forget it. It's not that simple.

Position, ownership of the spade suit, the psychological makeup of your opponents, the texture of your hand, the price tag on a possible sacrifice—all these factors must be considered, and will be discussed in this book. But for the present, here are a few pointers to tide you over.

When you have a part score, don't open with a poor suit. If you open four-card majors, make downright certain they are good four-card majors (A K J x or A Q J 10 or better). The reason is simple: partner is likely to stretch a point or two in an attempt to convert the partial. With J x x and as little as three points, even the experts are tempted into a single raise. The result can be disastrous.

Don't open a minimum hand with a "short club." All you will do is invite the opponents to a bidding party. Depending on your position, either lie low or open a weak notrump.

Responder should be equally concerned with having a good suit. If it converts the partial, he may well be stuck in the suit he responds in. For this reason, with balanced or semibalanced "dog meat," he should respond one notrump with anywhere from 4 to 12 points. When you own a partial, delicate "approach" bidding becomes a luxury of the idle rich.

The important thing to remember if you want the gods to smile on you in a money game is to watch the score with proper reverence. The score will dictate when, and how, you should crowd the odds and when you should accept them as the occasional misfortunes of war.

Position...
And Other
Pragmatic Pointers

Bridge, like a woman, is a fickle thing. To reduce either to a simple mathematical formula is downright ridiculous. Bridge experts know enough to leave the fair sex alone, but, Lord, how they try to reduce the game to arithmetic set in cement.

What started all this mathematical mumbo-jumbo was the Milton C. Work Point Count, whereby an ace was assigned the value of four points; a king, three; a queen, two; and a jack, one. Very simple, easily memorized. All that remained was to assign points for distribution. This the experts proceeded to do, and simplicity went out the window.

Fortunately, several million bridge players never

or rarely noticed. They were as happy as clams. They assigned three points for a void, two points for a singleton, one point for a doubleton, one or two points for each card more than four in the trump suit. When faced with a singleton king or a doubleton queen, they either whacked a point off or double-counted if they felt bearish. Rather than fuss with honor-trick tables, they happily attributed the same value to an ace and a king-jack.

A few thoughtful bridge players knew better, but their attempts to restore horse sense to the game resulted mostly in more, rather than less, arithmetic.

If this sounds as if I advocate the abandonment of point-counting—not at all. I swear by it . . . as long as it is accompanied by trick-counting.

Throughout this book point values are assigned to hands on the following basis:

> The usual 4–3–2–1 for ace, king, queen, jack
> One point for each trump more than four
> One point for a four-card side suit and 2 points for a five card side suit (count only one side suit, please)
> Zero points for a singleton king, queen, or jack—until reassured by partner's response that they may be worth something
> Zero points for a doubleton queen or jack—again until partner is heard from

One point for possession of a five-card spade suit

If this valuation seems too conservative, read on. You will learn a new kind of daring—prudent daring. You will have to throw some of your pet point-count notions into the trash can, but your friends will rate your game as anything but conservative.

SEVEN EiGHT NiNE!

For instance, you will find yourself opening one spade without batting an eyelash on ♠ A K Q 10 x x ♡ x x x x ◇ x x ♣ x. Only nine points in high cards, but a gold mine in the "noble suit." Your no-trump openings, as you have already seen in the preceding chapter, will amaze (and impoverish) your friends.

Prudent daring involves a brand-new look at most of the bids you now make automatically. Let's start with your opening bids.

"Do you play a Short Club?" This question is almost a ritual greeting between strangers at the bridge table. And whenever I hear it from a partner, it strikes cold fear in my heart. I know that I'm about to be subjected to "dog-meat" openings that convey more information to the opponents than to me. I know that in fourth position my partner will welcome the opposition into the bidding with open arms, until they steal the contract. I know that I had better sandbag in first or second position in the slim hope that I can hammer the enemy with a surprise double. I know that I'm playing with a partner who wouldn't open a decent four-card major if his life depended on it. If your hackles are beginning to rise, let me hasten to assure you that I, too, play a Short Club—and a Short Diamond, for that matter—but I see no reason to befuddle my partners by announcing it. I reserve the right to bid it only when it serves my purpose to do so. I will never submit voluntarily to a straitjacket.

The purpose of a short club (it doesn't deserve to be capitalized) is to make it easy for your partner to enter the auction. You are saying, in effect, "Don't just sit there, partner. Bid something." Either you have two rotten major suits and need support in one of them, or you have a modest "rockcrusher" (15 to

22 points). If he declines your invitation or if the opponents get into the act right away, fine. You have the wherewithal in the majors or in notrump to deal with them. In other words, it rarely pays to open a short minor unless your hand is rich in the majors or in defensive tricks.

With balanced or semibalanced garbage, it usually pays to pass. With ♠ Q 10 x ♡ K J x ◇ J 9 x ♣ A Q x x or ♠ K x x ♡ K J x x ◇ A x x ♣ Q x x in first position, I would recommend a quick pass even though both hands qualify as minimum opening bids under most systems. Minimum suit bids when you are playing for folding money should usually be supported by three defensive tricks in your side suits. With a decent major suit (A Q J 10 x, K Q J x x, A K 10 x x x, or better) you can forgo such caution. You have enough potential on attack to lessen your defensive requirements.

In a nutshell, THINK TRICKS, not points, before you open your mouth. In first or second position, especially, silence is golden.

Why is position so important? Why should it affect your vocal cords? The answer defies a systemic approach, yet it can be approached systematically. Perhaps the clearest way to explain the importance of position is to define the bidding objectives of each position as viewed by the money player.

First position: Your primary objective in opening one

of anything is to probe for a game—not for a partial. Don't open if game depends on partner's coming up with much more ammunition than you possess. To open, you need either a solid four-card suit, a decent five-card suit, or 15 good points.

Second position: Your objective is still game, but you can lower your requirements a little. With one opponent presumably too weak to open, you can open on 14 good points or the prospect of five or six tricks in a suit contract.

Third position: Besides game, your objectives are (1) to indicate a favorable opening lead for your partner, (2) to slow down the opponents' march toward a slam, (3) to indicate the best suit for a profitable save, and (4) to preempt the opponents out of the bidding altogether. Third position does not grant you a license to bid on mangy holdings just to reopen the bidding. You must have one of the above objectives clearly in mind before stepping into the fray.

Fourth position: Your objective is primarily a salvage operation and secondarily a probe for game. Contrary to popular belief, you don't need a "rock-crusher" to reopen the bidding. All you need is the best hand at the table, which is very likely if you have a legitimate opening bid. With three defensive tricks it is highly unlikely that passed opponents can get together in a game contract. With a five-card spade suit and 13 good points, go after a partial. With a five-card heart suit you need a slightly better hand. With a five-card minor suit and good stoppers in the side suits, you are generally better off opening a notrump and running like a thief to your long suit if doubled. The point is that in fourth position you must make every effort to force the opposition to enter the auction at the two level.

This last point brings up a basic principle, which should guide you in all positions: With a good hand, make it easy for your opponents to enter the auction; with an indifferent hand, make it as hard for them to bid as you safely can. This principle applies "in spades" when a partial exists either your way or theirs. With this in mind, let's look at a few hands and consider how you should bid them according to where you're sitting.

FIRST POSITION

♠ A x   ♡ A J 9 x x   ♢ A x x   ♣ Q x x

The texture of your five-card major suit is terrible. Open one notrump, especially when you own a 60 partial. You may freeze out an opponent's spade bid.

♠ A K Q J x x   ♡ x x   ♢ x x x   ♣ x x

Only 10 points in high cards, but the spade suit

is worth an extra point, and you've got six of them. If there is going to be a bidding duel, it pays to notify your partner right away that you have the best suit at the table. Bid one spade.

♠ Q J 9 x   ♡ J 10 x   ◇ A Q x   ♣ A J x

Without a partial your way, bid one spade and probe for a 4–4 fit to freeze out hearts. With a 60 partial to convert, you're better off opening one notrump to avoid the danger of your partner's stretching to raise you with x x x and 4 points.

♠ Q J x x   ♡ K Q x   ◇ x x x   ♣ A K J

My choice here is a diamond. You have the side suits nicely stopped, and if you are ever going to wind up in notrump, you will need spirited support from your partner in the suit that is missing from your hand.

♠ A K x   ♡ K Q x   ◇ x x   ♣ A Q J x x

Bid one club. You don't mind a little company in the bidding; and with a 90 partial your way, you will probably get it, much to your opponents' sorrow.

♠ x x   ♡ K Q x x   ◇ Q 10   ♣ A Q x x x

Pass like a shot. You are temporarily outgunned. If partner shows anything, you can always compensate for your silence.

♠ K Q x ♡ 10 9 x x x ◇ A K ♣ K x x

Bid one notrump. A heart bid might inflame your partner if he holds one of the four missing honors. In second position, with one opponent passed, you don't need a full sixteen points for an opening notrump bid.

♠ A K Q J ♡ x x ◇ K Q 10 x x ♣ A x

You are less interested now in freezing out the opposition, so why not describe the shape of your hand. Bid one diamond. Your hand is strong enough to merit a minor-suit opening.

♠ Q J 9 x x ♡ A x x ◇ K x x ♣ A x

An "automatic" bid of one spade, but only because your ragged suit is compensated for by two and a half defensive tricks in your side suits.

♠ x x ♡ A K Q J x x x ◇ A x x ♣ x

Bid four hearts, vulnerable or not. With five potential losers, you need a small fortune in partner's hand to make slam and you have a good chance to block a spade game if the hand belongs to the opposition.

50

♠ A x x ♡ Q x x x ◇ J x x ♣ A x x

A mangy heart suit that you don't particularly want your partner to lead dictates a pass. The only time you should be tempted to bid with this kind of hand is when you have a 60 partial not vulnerable against timid opponents. Then keep your fingers crossed and bid one notrump.

♠ x x ♡ x x x ◇ K Q J 10 x x ♣ K Q

Bid in anticipation of your opponents' eventually gaining the contract. You want diamonds led, so bid one diamond vulnerable. Bid three diamonds not vulnerable and throw a monkey wrench into the opponents' bidding machinery.

♡ A K Q J x x ◇ x ♣ A J x x

Bid four hearts. Your object is to prevent the opposition from finding a spade fit. In first position my bid would be two hearts.

♠ x x ♡ A x x ◇ A K ♣ K Q J 10 x x

With a 40 partial, I would bid three clubs, inviting the enemy to the funeral pyre if they compete, or eliciting a nice double if they let me "buy" the contract at the four level.

♠ Q 10 x ♡ K J 10 x x ◇ A Q x ♣ J 10

Don't throw it in—bid one heart. In fourth position you are in the perfect spot to snag a partial. After three passes, probabilities and plain common sense indicate that with even a minimum opening bid you hold the best hand at the table. The odds are even that partner will hold three-card support for your heart suit, and 73.5 times out of 100 he will hold at least 7 points in high cards. The only situation that might tempt you to toss this hand into the deadwood is when the opponents have a 40 partial. They might be able to steal the auction for two spades.

♥ J 10 9 x x ♡ A Q ◇ A x ♣ J x x x

Don't pitch this one. Bid one spade for the same reasons you bid one heart on the preceding hand and for the added reason that you control the spade suit.

♠ x x x x ♡ Q x ◇ A x x x ♣ A Q J

Pass with a sigh of relief. You have no defense against a major-suit contract. Opening a short minor on this sort of holding can only serve to awaken sleeping giants.

♠ A J x ♡ Q J x ◇ x x x ♣ A K 10 x

Now you can bid one club and find out where the diamonds are. You have both majors nicely stopped. With a 60 partial your way, however, take a modest risk and bid one notrump.

♠ K 10 9   ♡ K 10 9   ◇ A x x   ♣ K J 10 x

With or without a 60 partial not vulnerable, open one notrump. If the auction ends at notrump, you want the opening lead to—not through—your kings.

I hope these few examples will help to loosen up your bidding to a point where you are served rather than enslaved by mathematics. For further loosening up, I suggest you reread the chapter on partials. The aim of these two chapters has been to instill in you an approach to bidding that is logical enough, and elastic enough, to permit you to deal successfully with the fickle nature of bridge for blood. I call it prudent daring. You will call it money-in-the-bank once you're able to apply it properly.

Preempts
and Sacrifices
Without Tears

We have already examined a few price tags—the amounts you are willing to pay to prevent games and partials. Now let's go into more detail.

In almost every competitive endeavor the risk of loss is ever present. In bridge you must face this risk on every hand—and face it bravely. Unless you are dealt thirteen spades, every opening bid entails some risk. Every response entails some risk, either of faulty communication or of over optimism.

If you aren't occasionally doubled and set 500 or 800 points, you aren't playing bridge. Risk and loss are inevitable accompaniments of the game. But if this sounds like a plea for self-immolation, read on.

There is a vast difference between *reckless* spending and *investment* spending. The expert money bridge player spends points that the opponents chalk up above the line as an investment in the returns the odds will instantly or inevitably bring him.

An instant return, for example, is the difference between going down two doubled not vulnerable and letting the opponents score an ice-cold vulnerable game.

An inevitable return is what you get by being scrappy over partials. In the long run you will come out ahead. As I have said before, a part score is worth fighting for.

There are basically two ways to do investment spending at the card table: by preempting immediately or by outbidding eventually.

Preempting is not necessarily a giant leap to the three or four level. An opening bid at the one level or a single raise can have a preemptive effect. These little preempts are widely misunderstood by the addicts of the short club and by the responders who habitually reply one notrump to a major-suit opening bid with three-card trump support.

We have already dealt with the short-club addict in the previous chapter. Now let's give the poor responder a few lumps.

With ♠ J x x   ♡ x x x   ◇ K x x   ♣ A x x x, a one notrump response to partner's opening spade bid is accurate but ineffective if the opponents have a partial. Bid two spades and force them to do battle at the three level.

With a 40 partial your way and as little as ♠ x x x ♡ A x ◇ x x x x ♣ x x x x raise partner's opening one-spade bid in as calm a voice as you can. Two spades gives you only a slim chance of converting the partial if partner has bid with a minimum, but it gives you an excellent chance of severing enemy communications or of setting up partner for a profitable double if they intervene and he happens to have bid with a maximum.

The "approach" responder is another culprit who ignores the preemptive value of his hands. Opposite a one-heart opening with ♠ x x x ♡ K J 10 x ◇ A Q J x x ♣ x, he will invariably reply two diamonds "to convey a little more information." In my opinion, this is a blabbermouth bid. It does convey information, enough information to enable the opposition to probe for a possible save in one of the black suits. The only proper response is an immediate jump to four hearts.

This last example illustrates a curious paradox about bidding in bridge for blood: the object of 99 per cent of your bids is to reveal the nature of your hand to your partner and yet conceal it from your opponents. The more "approach" bidding you do, the less you conceal. When you find a fit with your partner or when you know instantly where the contract should eventually wind up, reveal this knowledge right away with a jump in his suit, or a jump in notrump if that is where the hand belongs.

The simplest, most direct way to reveal or conceal and to indicate where the hand should play, is via an opening preemptive bid—a terribly abused and misunderstood bid.

Deal the average player ♠ x ♡ A K Q J x x x- x x x ◇ x x, and once he recovers from the initial shock, he will open with four hearts and be hugely surprised when the opponents make either a profitable save or a small slam in spades. With only three losers in the hand, he should open five hearts (or four notrump if he can safely assume his partner will recognize it as Blackwood). The point illustrated by this hand is that you should always credit your partner with at least one trick in calculating the price you might have to pay for preempting.

The average player has a foggy notion that every time he holds a seven-card suit and less than an opening bid in high cards, he should open three of something. He may limit the bid further by insisting that the contract not exceed the makable tricks by more than two or three, depending on vulnerability. Preemptive openings are not that simple.

In the first place, you don't need seven cards in a major suit to preempt effectively. With ♠ x x x ♡ K Q J 9 x x ◇ x ♣ A x x, you should open three hearts, if not vulnerable, and try to freeze out a spade contract by the opposition. In third position, opposite a passed partner, this is a low-cost insurance policy.

Also, in third position with ten or eleven cards in the minors and a good hand, it pays to take out similar insurance, especially if you have a partial. Opposite a passed partner with ♠ x ♡ x x ◇ A K J 10 9 ♣ A Q J x x, open three clubs. You have no defense against a major-suit contract, and if you are doubled for business in your first suit, you can duck into your second at the same level.

Normally, when you open three in a minor, your bid should invite your partner to proceed to three notrump if he has solid stoppers in the side suits. It should promise a long solid suit that can be established with the loss of only one trick, and the hand

58

should contain at least one stopper or entry card on the side. The reason for limiting the bid in this way is simple: an opening three-club or three-diamond bid has practically no preemptive value if the opponents are loaded for bear in the majors. In first or second position a preemptive bid shouts of weakness. In third position against timid, vulnerable opponents, it may have some effect, but it may also have an inflammatory effect on your partner. He may take a chance on three notrump. You will be badly mauled if you can't deliver a suit as advertised.

Preempts are an attempt to outbid your opponents immediately with a minimum of risk. The risk involved in outbidding them eventually in a competitive auction depends on your partnership, the opponents' bidding and playing skill, and the price tag.

A good partnership determines a fit between two hands as rapidly as possible. Often overlooked in this process is the assigning of distribution points to the responder's hand. In a suit contract, a void is worth five points; a singleton, three; a doubleton, one. When responder has goodies like these, plus trump support, his first obligation is to announce it loud and clear. Eventually this knowledge—not the possession of miscellaneous aces and kings—will determine whether the partnership can profitably outbid the enemy.

Assessing the opponents' bidding and playing skill is not always easy, but always remember that even a deaf, dumb, and blind opponent can occasionally turn up with the right defense. Assume that the price you may have to pay will be the maximum.

We have already touched on price tags and how they are influenced by vulnerability and the existence of part scores. So you should have a rough idea of why the prices change. For instance, with neither side vulnerable and no partials, you are willing to spend 400 points on an average to prevent the opponents from making game. This means that if you

are doubled, you will shell out 300 points half the
time and 500 points the other half. If you have game
and a 60 partial and the opponents have game and
no partial, you should be willing to spend more.
Because of the edge your partial gives you, it is now
worth 700 points to prevent an adverse game.

Itemizing the amounts you should be willing to
spend in different tactical situations is difficult, but
not impossible, and it's probably the simplest way to
demonstrate the basic difference between tournament bridge and bridge for blood. "How much?"
That is the question.

	The maximum number of points you should spend to stop an
The situation	*ice-cold contract*

YOU: 0
THEY: 0

They bid for a partial of 30 or better	200-300
They bid game	400
They bid a small slam	700

YOU: 0
THEY: 60

They bid one notrump or better (game)	400
They bid a small slam	700

YOU: 0
THEY: Game

They bid for a partial of 30 or better	200-300
They bid game	500
They bid a small slam	900

YOU: 0
THEY: Game and 60
  They bid one notrump
    or better (game)   300
  They bid a small slam   800

YOU: 60
THEY: 0
  They bid for a partial of
    30 or better   200-300
  They bid game   500
  They bid a small slam   900

YOU: 60
THEY: 60
  They bid one notrump or
    better (game)   500
  They bid a small slam   900

YOU: 60
THEY: Game
  They bid for a partial of
    30 or better   200-300
  They bid game   500
  They bid a small slam   900

YOU: 60
THEY: Game and 60
  They bid one notrump or
    better (game)   400-500
  They bid a small slam   900

YOU: Game
THEY: 0
  They bid for a partial of
    30 or better   200
  They bid game   500
  They bid a small slam   800

YOU: Game
THEY: 60
  They bid one notrump or
    better (game)   400-500
  They bid a small slam   800

YOU: Game
THEY: Game
  They bid for a partial of
    30 or better   200
  They bid game   500
  They bid a small slam   1100

YOU: Game
THEY: Game and 60
  They bid one notrump or
    better (game)   400-500
  They bid a small slam   800

YOU: Game and 60	
THEY: 0	
They bid for a partial of	
30 or better	100-200
They bid game	500
They bid a small slam	800
YOU: Game and 60	
THEY: 60	
They bid one notrump or	
better (game)	500
They bid a small slam	800
YOU: Game and 60	
THEY: Game	
They bid for a partial of	
30 or better	200
They bid game	700
They bid a small slam	1100
YOU: Game and 60	
THEY: Game and 60	
They bid one notrump or	
better (game)	500
They bid a small slam	1100

Several items in the chart bear explanation. Some of the price tags do not exist in the scoring tables. For example, a set of 700 vulnerable doesn't happen. In arriving at this figure I considered that part of the time you will pay less than the full price, thanks to poor defense or timid opponents.

Don't pay top dollars to prevent a partial against good opponents. The time to shell out 300 points is when you are reasonably certain that you hold a healthy edge in bidding and play.

A partial of 20 is usually useless. It can come in handy, however, when you hold a good hand and open preemptively to convert it.

Missing from the chart is the price you should pay to stop a grand slam. My advice is to take your licking like a soldier, except in the rare instances when you can find a save in a major suit without cutting off your nose. As a rule of thumb, I consider the price tag for a grand slam roughly equivalent to that for a small slam in the above situations.

Finally, keep a running balance sheet in your head. Obviously, it isn't worth 500 points to stop a game if you have already paid that price to stop a previous game. Determine who has the edge above the line before you sacrifice.

DOUBLE
TROUBLE

The most abused bid in bridge is "Double!" A few of its variations are: "I double." (Don't take me out of it or I'll slit your throat.) "Double three spades." (We've really got 'em hammered in this suit.) "Double?" (What do you think, partner?) "I'll crack that." (They're down at least three.) "I'll give that a touch." (They've got a fighting chance.) "Play for eight spades." (Hope you can stand the sight of blood, partner.)

As chairman of the Ethics Committee of the Chicago and North Western Bridge and Bourbon Society (a commuter group distinguished by a somewhat casual attitude toward the rules and proprieties

of the game) the only version of the bid I will toler-
ate is a soft-spoken "Double." Of course, if the train
is crowded and the noise level intense, then
"DOUBLE!" is perfectly O.K. On occasion I have
delivered the bid in tones calculated to shatter glass,

but only because I have had to outshout an impassioned post-mortem across the aisle.

The true abuse of the double, however, is its misuse.

I have seen actuaries, soybean speculators, loan sharks, and successful horseplayers double a vulnerable 90 partial in hopes of setting it one trick.

To gain 100 points they were perfectly willing to give the opposition a chance to make 930 points (180 for contract, 50 for the insult, and 700 for the rubber). At the track, this is like putting the mortgage money on a horse that will pay only $2.20 to win for a $2 ticket. Since only a third of the favorites come in first, this is mathematical idiocy. So, too, in bridge—only more so.

Then there is the matter of the "free" double of a game contract. "Free," my foot. Here your attempt to gain 50 or 100 extra points gives your opponents an extra 170 points in a major suit if they make it. You're still on the losing end of the bid. You lose even more if your double gives them enough information to make the contract, in which case you buck odds of 3 to 1. And if your "free" double brings rain in the form of a successful redouble, you're bucking odds that can exceed 10 to 1.

Does this mean you should turn in your doubling shoes and sit like a mouse at the card table? Not at all. It simply means that you must consider the profit motive at all times: When you double, your profit must exceed the value of any contract you might be able to make.

A corollary to this rule of thumb is don't make dubious doubles when you have a sure sacrifice. As you have seen (I hope) from the previous chapter, sensible sacrificing brings sure profits in the long run.

Sucker doubles can cost you a fortune, but a fortune can slip through your fingers if you do *not* double. How can you tell when silence is golden and when it is not? Here are a few guidelines:

With an intelligent partner and length in the opponents' trump suit, you can afford to gamble with low-level doubles.

By an "intelligent" partner I mean one who is as profit-minded as you. If he sees a greater profit elsewhere, he will treat your double as only a tentative invitation to a slaughter. He will take you out of your double if all he needs is a little specific information from you to make a game or even a slam. Don't sulk —show your stuff.

The reason you need trumps—either a lot of them for nuisance value or solid tricks for your set— is clear. When you double at a low level, you are in effect playing the hand in the opponents' suit.

When partner makes an opening bid, you usually deduce that he has two or three defensive tricks.

When an opponent overcalls, you add these tricks to your own potential defensive tricks and assess the possibility of a profitable double. Without trumps, however, your partner's tricks and yours can become very, very dubious. If you haven't many trumps, obviously the opponents are loaded with them. You can safely infer that your partner's opening bid was largely distributional. If you have trump support for his suit, that support becomes virtually worthless on defense. One of your opponents is bound to have a singleton or a void. Figure also that if your defensive tricks are clustered in a long suit of your own, they, too, can founder on the rocks of distribution.

The ideal double of a low-level minor-suit bid should be based on about 10 good points, little relish for your partner's suit, and at least one trump trick. To double a low-level major-suit bid, you should have almost an opening bid, no long major suit of your own, and, hopefully, two trump tricks. The prospect of doubling opponents into game should not be taken lightly.

Don't double little old ladies who have blundered into a game contract unless you can infer from the bidding that the cards are sitting badly for them.

This long-winded maxim covers a large territory.

In the first place, it rarely pays to double poor, timid players who bid game: chances are they have

slam and one of them has underbid throughout the auction out of fear or outright ignorance. I much prefer to double experts who have made four or five "scientific" bids to arrive at game. To be sure, they have made their holdings explicit to their partners, but they have also given me a blueprint that tells me and my partner exactly where to place the bomb.

For instance, consider this "expert" bidding sequence:

OPENER	RESPONDER
1 ♠	1 NT
2 ♡	2 ♠
3 ♠ (Maybe we have game.)	4 ♠ (Let's try.)

From this sequence it is apparent that responder has no stomach for opener's secondary suit. He has miserable trump support. Opener doesn't have the stuff for a jump rebid. Thus, if you hold ♡ K J 10 x ◇ Q J 10 x ♣ A J 10 x x, by all means double. Don't let the void in the trump suit deter you from a high-level double. In effect, you are playing the contract at notrump. The missing trumps are undoubtedly sitting in your partner's hand and you have the other suits nicely blocked.

The principle here is devastatingly simple: the more you know about card locations that the opponents don't know, the more likely your double will

73

draw blood. This is why lurking in the bushes with moderate strength and dim prospects of game pays off. If you constantly overcall or make takeout doubles just to hear the sound of your own voice, you discourage opponents from the ultimate folly—a shoddy game contract. Lie low until you can give them an unpleasant surprise. In rubber bridge the unpleasant surprise should always be based on the expectation of hammering the opponents two tricks—not one. Always bear this in mind. Maybe it will prevent your doubling strictly on your partner's bidding. Unless you have some strength of your own, you may be handing the opponents a pleasant surprise.

Points alone do not a double make.

The worst bleat you can hear from a partner after the opponents have racked up a redoubled contract is, "But I had 14 points and you bid, buddy."

Consider this auction:

SOUTH	WEST (You)	NORTH	EAST
1 ♡	1 ♠	4 ♡	?

If East doubles with ♠ K x x x ♡ Q J ◇ K Q x x x ♣ Q J, don't let him call you "buddy" any more. He is an unwitting foe.

The occasions when points are virtually meaningless are fairly easy to spot. Confident bidding

74

when a fit is quickly established should tip you off. If it doesn't tip your partner off, take him out of his double if you have a reasonable save, and then insist that he listen to the post-mortem as you explain exactly why his points weren't worth a damn on defense. Normally I detest post-mortems, but point-happy partners have to be dealt with, unless you can afford to drum them out of your games.

Don't double the only contract you can set.

For instance, you hold ♠ x x ♡ Q J 10 x ◇ A x ♣ x x x x x. After much backing and filling, the opponents bid six hearts and the bid rolls around to you in the last bidder's seat. If you double, you should have your head examined. What good are your sure heart tricks if they can rattle off twelve tricks at six notrump? All your opponents need for this contract are the ace and king of hearts and ten tricks from their side suits. Not at all improbable half the time you encounter this situation, and it has to occur only one time out of twenty to hand you a loss.

The above example is elementary. Much more complex choices may confront you. Just bear in mind that all avenues of escape must be safely blocked before you double. This is especially important in doubling slam contracts. I never double slams unless I am playing with a partner who is familiar with Mr. Lightner's lead-directing double. In which case I double, because it is the only way I have of defeating the contract and saving our side a bundle of points. The double usually indicates an ability to ruff and requests an abnormal lead from partner, usually his longest suit. Unfortunately, partners who have heard about Mr. Lightner are scarcer than warts on a billiard ball. Most partners don't understand all the other lead-directing doubles available to a trained partnership either. So I usually double expecting the worst lead possible.

So much for maxims. Let's consider another abused, confused double: the takeout double. The notion persists that a takeout double must guarantee support for any and all of the unbid suits. The notion persists especially among so-called Goren players who haven't taken the trouble to read Mr. Goren's latest works. He now makes the bid a great deal more flexible. Of necessity, because the lopsided hands that formerly rated a strong jump overcall have to find a niche. The jump overcall in current Goren is now reserved for long-suited hands that offer dim prospects for game. For example, with ♠ Q J 10 x x x ♡ x x ◇ x x x ♣ K Q, bid two spades over an opposing opening bid of one in hearts, diamonds, or clubs. The bid serves nicely as a monkey wrench in the opponents' bidding machinery.

With a strong lopsided holding where all you need is a little information to take the plunge to game, you can either cue-bid or bid a takeout double. With ♠ A K J 10 x x ♡ A Q J ◇ x ♣ x x x over an opening bid of one diamond, you double. If partner responds in clubs, you've got it made. He has filled a major chink in your armor. If he responds with anything else, you indicate your good fortune in spades and see if you forced him to respond with a bust. With only slight encouragement game is almost a certainty.

A two-suited hand shouldn't deter you from a takeout double either. With the following bidding sequence:

SOUTH	WEST	NORTH	EAST
1 ◇	Pass	1 ♠	Double

all East needs for his takeout double is a willingness to compete in one of the unbid suits. All he needs to know from his partner is which suit. Not vulnerable, East can hold as little as ♠ x x ♡ Q J 10 x x ◇ x ♣ K J 10 x x. Obviously the opponents have the tickets, but a profitable save may be in order.

Purists may hoot at this use of a takeout on the theory that the "unusual" notrump covers this situation. If your partner plays this convention and you have agreed that the unusual notrump covers the unbid suits, this is peachy. But partners who are familiar with this particular convention with all its rami-

fications are rare indeed. Stick with your clumsy, old-fashioned double and you can't go wrong. Unless, that is, your partner takes it for a business double. In which case you have my heartfelt sympathy.

Another notion that persists about the takeout double is that if you double one major, you must have solid support for the other major if your partner bids it. This, for my money, is a nicety reserved for the tournament tables. With one or two good minor suits and fine prospects of game, I'll double a major for information any time. If you don't agree, talk to my accountant.

Another double that leads to trouble is the double of a preemptive bid. Dubbed the "co-operative" double, it usually produces anything but co-operation. Partner has to guess wherein the greatest profit lies: at game or in racking up a nice penalty. Most partners have difficulty in choosing the correct alternative. They invariably name a trashy four-card suit, especially if they are short in the opponents' trump suit. It never occurs to them that your double might be based in part on a nicely situated trump holding.

With a good partner there is little cause for confusion. He will deduce from my double the following: (1) that I hold a minimum of four or five defensive tricks, (2) that I don't have a solid suit of my own that could produce game or I would have bid it, and (3) that I don't have a giant hand with a double-stopper in the opponents' suit or I would have bid three notrump.

With a long, worthless suit he can figure that some of my defensive tricks will evaporate through ruffing and that he should bail us out of the double. With defensive tricks in short suits he knows enough to sit back and lick his chops. With a giant hand of his own he can smell slam for our side and bid accordingly.

With a poor partner I know for certain that these inferences are impossible. I insist that we employ a gimmick method of dealing wtih preempts. I will play Fishbein, cheaper minor, or notrump for takeout, in that order of preference.

Fishbein is a calculated risk because most partners who attempt to use it bid three notrump over an opening three-spade bid and wonder why I pass (four clubs is the takeout bid under the original Fishbein convention). They also forget that Fishbein applies only in the direct position—not in the reopening position. I know that in fourth seat with a dandy suit that could be misconstrued as a Fishbein bid, if I overcalled in it, I must fold my tent and silently steal away. However, something is better than nothing. At least I have the chance to inflict a penalty double against poor opponents who preempt with long but badly textured suits.

Cheaper minor and notrump are less risky because the players who are familiar with these conventions are somewhat more sophisticated than the players who think they are familiar with the Fishbein Convention. Both conventions are abominations, to my way of thinking. Cheaper minor commits you to exchanging information at a perilously high level. Notrump I don't like, because all too often I want to play the hand at three notrump and all I need from my partner is silence.

A sadly neglected form of the double is the redouble—a beautiful bid in the right hands. Unfortunately, it is a catastrophic bid in the wrong hands. I will rarely let my partner's redouble stand if he is an overoptimistic boob or a rich duplicate player. I will run to any hole I can find.

Another danger of the redouble in the wrong hands is that partner's redoubles of an ice-cold contract may send the opponents scurrying into a save at a level where our contract would founder.

The beauty of the bid lies in the golden harvest it can bring you and the panic it can produce in your opponents.

A redoubled major-suit contract at the four level made on the nose lands you a bonus of 240 points over and above the profit you receive from making a doubled contract. Not a fortune exactly. Your bonus for making four of a minor redoubled is only 160 points. Not really worth the mental anguish if your contract is at all dubious.

The cash register begins to play a heavenly tune, however, when overtricks enter the scene. Given a 50–50 chance of going down one vulnerable or of making your contract with an overtrick, the money odds are:

4 ♠	redoubled with an overtrick	+930
4 ♠	doubled with an overtrick	+490
4 ♠	redoubled down one	—400
4 ♠	doubled down one	—200

The redouble nets you a gain of 440 points against the possible loss of only 200 extra points. With such odds it pays to plunge, but only when you are in a position to maul the opposition badly if they try to deprive you of your golden opportunity by bidding a suit of their own.

The true glitter of the redouble, for my money, lies in the panic it can produce and the putrid contracts it can drive your opponents into, especially at the lower levels of bidding. For instance, consider this bidding sequence:

NORTH	EAST	SOUTH (You)	WEST
1 ♠	Double	Redouble	?

If you are holding ♠ x ♡ A J 10 x ◇ K 10 9 8

82

♣ Q J 10 9, you hand West a nifty pickle. Any suit he bids is bound to break badly for him. This can lead to a chain reaction of bidding, with the level rising higher and higher as your opponents frantically try to find a fit. You will note in this hand that you have no support for your partner's suit. You don't have to. As a matter of fact, your partner has no right to expect it. With support for his suit and a game-going hand, you would have made another bid. In effect, your redouble tells him, "Partner, we don't have game, but we do have an excellent chance for a nice, juicy penalty." If the opponents don't take the bait, and partner's suit is not self-sufficient, he should bail out of the redouble.

In this chapter we have dealt lightly with partners: good one and bad ones. Read on, and we will deal with this subject in greater detail.

Partners,

and What to Do
About Them

A railroad strike in Chicago provided me with a surprising upturn in my fortunes at the card table. It also provided me with valuable experience in the management of partners.

Because Chicago was too far from the North Shore for a daily hike and because nobody in his right mind wanted to lock bumpers with all the other displaced commuters, the Chicago and North Western Bridge and Bourbon Society chartered a bus.

By knocking out a few seats we were able to provide for four tables of bridge in air-conditioned comfort. Out of sheer kindness we permitted a few

gin rummy players and newspaper readers to accompany us. The bus made several stops in the morning before hitting the expressway. But the bridge games started immediately, and we were assured of anywhere from forty minutes to an hour of uninterrupted play. At night the games usually lasted longer. We finished up in leisurely fashion on somebody's front lawn. On Fridays, after a long, hard week, we enjoyed the services of an accordionist and a lovely, leggy young lady in mesh leotards who sang and served cocktails.

It was a balmy summer in more ways than one. As a commuter, I never had it so good. As a bridge player, I lived in paradise on wheels. I thrive on unhinged opponents, and the wayward bus served my purposes admirably. The noise level was splendid. On Fridays it was deafening. The bus lurched and swayed through traffic like a spastic whale. And all the delightful chaos served to magnify the basic flaws of most of the players. Timid players became downright cowardly. Plungers started bidding as if money were going out of style. For a practical psychologist, such as myself, it was an illuminating experience.

Let me introduce you to some of my fellow passengers. (The names have been changed, of course. I'm still playing with these characters.)

First, let's meet "Chadwick Chicken." Chad is a corporation lawyer who wears rubbers and totes an umbrella when the weather forecast reads, "Partly cloudy and clearing." He prides himself on his play of the cards, and his pride is justified. He makes all *his* contracts—with overtricks—simply because he never bids enough. When his exasperated partner pushes him into something unmakable, he will invariably underbid the next five hands. As a partner, Chad is a challenge. Culbertson once suggested that the only way to deal with such a chronic underbidder is to underbid yourself—on the theory that, once reassured, the poor boob will turn brave. With Chad this is a forlorn hope.

I pull out all stops with Chad—praise, reassurance, coaching, respect, suspicion, and silent prayer.

When I cut him as partner, I always feign great joy. I greet him with a spiel that goes something like this: "Thank God I've got a card player for a partner. With your skill and my luck we should clobber these guys. Don't forget our motto, Chad baby, open light and overcall strong."

This nauseating banter is quite calculated. I am in hopes that, by praising his playing skill, I will get him to bid one more time on borderline hands because *he* is the declarer. The reference to my "luck" is another shoring-up device. I have managed to convince good old Chad that I'm the last of the great card-holders, and this often has a wondrous effect on his backbone when I am likely to end up playing the hand. Our "motto" is a myth. In a comradely way I'm reminding not to throw 14 perfectly good points into the deadwood in the pass-out position. I'm also giving him a specific area in which to practice his conservatism. I've noticed that, inconsistent as it may seem, timid players who are loath to open the bidding have no such compunctions when it comes to overcalling. Yet the overcall is the most dangerous bid in bridge. Whenever possible, I try to insist that my partners regard the bid with proper awe.

Early in the game with Chad I make one spec-
tacular underbid and then follow it with an elaborate
post-mortem pointing out what might have befallen
the hand if everything had been sitting wrong. This
is usually enough to convince Chad that I'm a fellow
card-carrying conservative. From then on I bid normally—almost.

When Chad gives me a single raise in my suit,
I become highly suspicious. Usually his bid is based
on indifferent trump support and good stuff in side
suits he is reluctant to mention. A rebid of two notrump smokes this information out. Chad breathes
a huge sigh of relief and bids three notrump. Whereupon I either clam up, even though I know full well
that the hand is being played from the wrong side
of the table, or, expecting the worst, I take the
plunge in my major.

Another bidding adjustment I make for Chad
is shading my third- and fourth-position opening
bids just a hair—especially when I hold a good suit
or two. This often brings Chad back amongst the
living.

Chad's opposite number is found in the person
of "Winnetka Fats." A fine card player, too, but a
chronic overbidder. An insurance adjuster by trade,
Fats weighs ninety pounds after a heavy meal and
carries the attitude to the table that everybody is
out to hornswoggle him. In a competitive auction he

is likely to see red and bid to the hilt out of sheer vindictiveness. He is constantly on the alert for a "psyche." (I always manage to throw one in when I'm his opponent.) An opponent's preempt throws him into an instant snit, and he will enter the auction with absolute dog meat. He is an almost incurable optimist when it comes to bidding games and slams. Culbertson's way of dealing with a bidder like Fats is to overbid, too, until he pulls in his horns. I prefer my own methods. I can't afford Culbertson's.

With Fats I am not above a little shock therapy. If his first contract is doubled, I'll redouble like a shot. Down two not vulnerable is a small price to pay for the sobering effect it has on him. To persist beyond this, however, is expensive folly. The cheapest way to deal with Fats and his kind is to project an image of absolute reliability in your bidding and to acquire an early lead even if that requires underbidding an almost sure slam. Paranoid partners invariably relax when they have a clear edge in the scoring column. Any capacity they may have for sound bidding is more likely to assert itself. Being even a momentary loser brings out the beast in them.

Another device that helps in dealing with over-bidders is to pass with borderline hands, and sometimes even with good ones. You know for certain that the overbidder will enter the auction if he has anything, and then you can safely show your stuff.

You will occasionally throw an ice-cold game into the deadwood as a result of this calculated conservatism. But throw your hand in fast, scramble the cards, complain about your square distribution, and go on to bigger and better things.

The toughest partner to deal with is "Marvin Mavin." A financial wizard in the factoring business, Marv was (and is) one of the biggest pigeons ever to sit down at a card table with money in mind. Yet if I were ever again to be roped into a duplicate tournament, I would unhesitatingly pick him for a partner. A squeeze, a dummy reverse, any coup you can think of, is mere child's play to good old Marv. His bidding is scientific to the nth degree. In the average auction, if you are an alert expert, his bids will indicate every pip in his hand. His bidding is so precise, so absolutely reliable (if you can understand all its subtleties), that Marv constantly reiterates a phrase now famous in Chicago bridge circles: "T.U.P." Literal translation: "Trost yo' potnr."

For perfectly good reasons, I wouldn't trust Marv in a money game if he had each bid notarized.

For all his science and skill, Marv has never mastered the difference between "How often?" and "How much?" His disregard of price tags is horrendous. His ignorance of partials is appalling. He overlooks either their existence or their value. His sacrifices are theoretically sensational, but practically suicidal.

What to do about Marv and his fellow experts? Simple. Mistrust them, but don't let them know it.

On borderline doubles, take them out every time. Invariably they are angling for a one-trick set with perfect defense. Dandy in duplicate, but dumb in rubber bridge. When you go down in your save, listen patiently to the angry post-mortem and apologize all over the rug. Never in your wildest dreams will you ever install a grain of horse sense into this kind of player.

Another self-protective device is bidding "dumb." When you have the choice of bidding something beautifully explicit or bidding something "dumb simple" that accurately describes the general nature of your hand, choose the latter bid. Let partner be the blabbermouth who helps the opponents find the winning defense. This deliberate obfuscation also puts a damper on partner's tendency to make a beautiful but costly sacrifice based on bidding inferences.

The best of all self-protective devices with a full-time duplicate player is sneaky but effective. Insist that he keep score. Your opening gambit in the game is, "For God's sake, let Marv keep score. He's the only one in the game who can add." With partials right under his snoot he will be much less likely to overlook them.

The other characters on the bus and the means to deal with them, should you come to Chicago are:

"Hal Haretrigger"—big butter-and-egg man and chronic doubler. (Don't you believe him.)

"Sol Sandbag"—corporate lawyer and foxy grampa who passes good stuff and then punishes you for bidding his cards in third or fourth position. (Don't shade your openings ever.)

"Orville Overtrick"—actuarial consultant and superb player who boots cold contracts trying for an overtrick. (Hog the bidding shamelessly.)

As I said, the wayward bus was very illuminating. It led me to compose the following checklist for sizing up partners—especially strangers. It may help you, too. Keep it a silent quiz, whenever possible, and you will prosper. It never pays to put a partner on the spot.

Does he want to play a short club? Be on guard. He may abuse it, but take comfort in the knowledge that his major-suit openings will indicate a five-card holding or better.

Does he play Stayman? Don't be too sure. This is a much abused convention. Suspect his two no-trump rebids. It may just indicate a putrid minimum with no stomach for a major. If he does not play Stayman, resign yourself to some ambiguity.

Did he suggest Fishbein over preempts? Something is better than nothing with poor players. Accept his terms, but assume he doesn't really understand the convention.

How badly did he mangle the first contract he played as declarer? Should you steer or hog the contracts so you can play them yourself? Bear in mind that a hacker in a cold contract is better than an expert in an impossible one.

Does he show any imagination on defense? If not, do something about his doubles. Go down one or two in a save contract.

Is he sophisticated enough to understand a forc-

ing pass . . . a Lightner double . . . an unusual notrump . . . a balancing double? It is downright stupid to make an intelligent bid opposite an ignoramus.

Is he afraid to make an opening bid? If so, watch out. Give him too much encouragement and he may make up for his previous silence by bidding you to oblivion.

Does he always count his cards after the deal to make sure he has thirteen? He's a duplicate player. This can be good or bad. Watch him like a hawk.

With friends it is fairly easy to keep a mental card file of idiosyncrasies. The point is: Don't fight them. Adjust. Don't preach. Don't teach. Suffer in silence and relax in the knowledge that "odds omnia vincit." If you let mathematics rather than emotions rule your game, eventually you will triumph.

CHICAGO,
the Name of the Game Is
MONEY

Chicago, four-deal bridge, is said to have originated in the Windy City in response to an alarming increase in homicides at the card table. Bridge players who habitually prolonged rubbers into Pyrrhic victories were reportedly dropping like flies. Senseless sacrificers who dropped thousands of points when not vulnerable against vulnerable opponents were dropping dead in droves, victims of instant lead poisoning.

Not true. Even the canard that Chicago is *the* Windy City (it is the nineteenth windiest in the nation).

The new version of four-deal bridge, however,

did eliminate the human nuisances mentioned above —peaceably. By arbitrarily assigning vulnerability to each hand and limiting the "rubber" to four hands —no more, no less—the game ruled out the possibility of being hopelessly stuck with a moron for a partner.

There were fringe benefits, too. Chicago set a new pace for rubber bridge: fast and furious. But the biggest benefit lay in the scoring. Because the rewards for a game are bestowed immediately (300 or 500 points) and because partials earned not vulnerable can apply one or two hands later to a vulnerable situation, the scores racked up are about 20 per cent higher than at garden variety rubber bridge. Whoopee! It's a beautiful game for the money-minded.

In case you aren't familiar with Chicago, here is how it goes:

First hand: Neither side vulnerable. Game is worth a 300-point bonus. Partials carry over to subsequent hands.

Second hand: Dealer's side vulnerable. Dealer's game is worth 500 points. Non-dealer's game is worth 300 points. Partials still carry over.

Third hand: Scored as for second hand. Partials still carry over.

Fourth hand: Both sides vulnerable. Partials are now worth trick score plus a 100-point bonus.

All other bonuses and penalties are scored exactly as at rubber bridge and according to vulnerability. Each of the four hands *must* be opened or redealt by the assigned dealer. The deal moves clockwise, and the rotation is indicated by a big fat **X** scrawled or printed at the top of the score pad.

1. indicates the first hand
   (neither side vulnerable)
2. indicates the second hand
   (dealer's side vulnerable)
3. indicates the third hand
   (dealer's side vulnerable)
4. indicates the fourth and final hand
   (both sides vulnerable)

(In New York's posh, plush Cavendish Club, where bridge's major leaguers compete for sometimes bloodcurdling stakes, nondealer's side is vulnerable on the second and third hands. A neat wrinkle that encourages dealer to preempt to the hilt to shut out or confuse vulnerable opposition.)

Sounds like a simple enough variation of good, old rubber bridge, doesn't it? Well, it isn't. The pace and the increased scoring opportunities can throw you for a loss, if you aren't careful. Here is a hand by hand analysis of the game and the tactics you should apply:

Don't get greedy. The immediate gain of 300 bonus points for a game can turn your head. It's real, real, real—not theoretical. Bid boldly and bravely, but not brashly. Prudent daring still applies. More important, an ironclad partial can come in very handy when you are vulnerable—and in Chicago it happens in a hurry.

If you are in third or fourth seat, fight like a tiger if you have a chance at a partial, rather than tossing in the towel and awaiting better fortune on a redeal. In this situation the gods and the odds favor the bold in spades—especially in spades. With good texture and only 10 points, open the bidding. A partial is worth at least 200 points whether you make one or prevent one.

Second hand: opponents vulnerable; you are not.

In this situation you are facing one of your opponents' two opportunities for a big vulnerable score. A spanner in their bidding machinery is clearly called for. In first or second position open light to indicate a suit worth sacrificing in, or consider a slightly dubious preempt in a well-textured, six-card minor suit with garbage on the side. In third seat, opposite a passed partner, you should preempt even on a fairly decent hand with predominantly minor-

100

suit strength. Remember, you can average a 600-point loss by stopping a vulnerable game (500 points and trick score) and still break even.

Fourth position in this situation really separates the men from the boys. With as few as eight high-card points and a good suit, swallow your fears and

open. Your object is to prevent a redeal in which your opponents have a great deal to gain and you have a great deal to lose. Take them off vulnerability even if it causes your nervous juices to jangle a little.

THIRD HAND: YOU ARE VULNERABLE; OPPONENTS ARE NOT.

Naturally, you stretch a little to reach game and cash in on your vulnerability. With a major suit and a reasonable doubt as to success or failure, go for the game. With a minor suit and little hope for game, bid as high as you can as fast as you can to snag a partial you might convert when vulnerable on the last hand. In fourth position with a mediocre hand, by all means pass. Try for a redeal and better luck.

FOURTH HAND: BOTH SIDES VULNERABLE.

Watch your step. Submerge any bulldog tendencies you may have carried over from ordinary rubber bridge. You can't make up for a stupid sacrifice on the next hand—this is it. Bid tight as wallpaper, unless you are ahead and have the best partner at the table, in which case you can loosen up a little and try for a quick and dirty profit. Remember, too, even your partials are worth less (trick score plus 100 points). They are no longer worth a theoretical 200 to 300 points.

Chicago, according to some experts, is "duplicate with partials." With this in mind, they recommend much looser, more liberal bidding than would be employed in normal rubber bridge. This is very dangerous advice. Horse sense and the constant self-questioning "How much will it cost me?" apply in Chicago as they never applied in duplicate. And this is what this little book is all about. Bear in mind the principles and the price tags we have already discussed and you can face your first session at Chicago unafraid.

Odds
&
Ends

The following is devoted to random ramblings and observations concerning the wonderful—and sometimes wacky—world of rubber bridge. It is, in an aphorism or two, a "Rich Richard's Almanac" of how to play bridge for blood.

When playing bridge on planes or trains, always pick an aisle seat.

I have known deacons and rabbis gifted with 20/20 peripheral vision. On a crowded commuter car a man needs the forbearance of a saint not to peek. Knowing human frailties as I do, I always make it a point to sit where peeking is difficult and where my cards won't be reflected in a window. I clutch them to my bosom, secure in the knowledge that I am not giving my opponents an unnecessary edge.

Know the rules.

It took me much too long to realize that ninety-nine bridge players out of a hundred haven't the foggiest idea of how the rules protect them. After failing to collect on hundreds of dollars' worth of angry verbal bets concerning what the rules did or did not say, I began to carry a copy of them in my overcoat on blustery winter days. The documentary evidence has paid for the overcoat many times over. It's just too damned bad I haven't lived through enough cold, wet summers. Somehow it seems downright silly to burden myself with an official copy of the ACBL rules when it's ninety degrees in the shade. At times like these I like to travel light.

Patience is sometimes a virtue.

With slow, stupid partners it most often pays to play a slow, stupid game. Your primary objective with a poor partner is to play as few hands as possible. This is hard to do. Invariably a poor partner will put you behind the eight-ball early in the game. And your natural tendency will be to bid and play faster in hopes of making up the deficit. Don't. When rape is inevitable, relax and enjoy it as much as you possibly can. Practice counting down opponents' hands. Recite your partner's more obvious virtues—maybe he was always kind to his sainted old mother, a chronic sufferer from Dutch elm disease. Depending on where you happen to be stuck, stare out the window of your train at the passing scene or mentally price the furniture in the poor boob's living room.

The important point to remember is that the more hands you play, the more you will lose.

Play fast when you can make a profit.

With a good partner your object is to cram as many hands as possible into the time you have to play. Concede the opponents' one-bids and cold contracts as speedily as you can. Threaten slow players with "lack of track" or pressing business elsewhere. Make quick claims for your contracts even though careful play might land you an overtrick or two. With "fish," time is money.

Fear the Greeks even bearing gifts.

One of the most unscrupulous sharks ever to sit down at a table is a character I dub "Gayelord Ravelsleeves." A classic auction with this unprincipled crumb went as follows:

Gayelord's partner: "Pass."
Long hesitation.
Gayelord: "One heart."

"Two spades."

The contract wound up in four spades, making five. Six hearts was absolutely cold. And what was Gayelord's holding? ♠ x x ♡ x x x ◇ J x x x x ♣ K x x. His one heart was an atrocious bid, but in third position our hero realized that by bidding out of turn he could bar his partner from the auction and throw a smelly red herring across the opponents' path. Result: Gayelord has trouble finding a game.

A variation of Gayelord's gambit is to make a deliberate underbid and then correct it in an imaginary suit. Partner is automatically barred forever from the auction, thereby making it impossible for the partnership to get into deeper water. Deplorable, but something to watch out for, lest someone pull it on you in a tough, rule-minded game.

Grant "friendly credit terms" if a sucker owes you money.

This may seem like misplaced generosity, but if he is a true sucker, he will have every confidence that he will recover his losses at the next session with the pasteboards. Encourage him by all means with "no money down and six months to pay." Losing psychology will almost invariably interfere with his bidding. Spurred by his previous losses, he will take more chances than a sick millionaire. Profit accordingly.

Play for no little stakes.

How much you play for is your business. Find a comfortable amount and *stick with it!* If big stakes for you are half a cent a point and you have the skill to back it up, don't settle for less. Shame, cajole, browbeat, or "one-up" your opponents into playing on your terms. There is nothing worse than winning at a tenth and losing at a half.

If the opposition won't play ball, try side bets— as many and as complicated as you can make. Eventually you can suggest an upped ante instead of "all these absurd bets I can't possibly manage to keep track of."

Do not be an optimist.

According to the probability tables there is no such thing as luck after one hundred deals. True enough, *but—* There is no reason to suspect after

fifty poor deals that the fifty-first will bring you good fortune. The same inexorable odds exist on finesses and distribution. Don't fritter away good cards or buck miserable ones because "the odds are bound to change." They won't.

Losers lose on a hundred hands because they beat themselves by ignoring eternal verities and by playing badly. Losing psychology gets them that way.

A "bug" should be avoided like the plague.

Some people you just cannot play with—either as opponents or as partners. For one reason or another they bring out the worst in your game and your disposition. If you can't gracefully avoid them, at least cut your stakes in half. Life is too short to lose money this way.

Don't hum off-key when playing against music lovers.

There are enough ways to irritate opponents without being an utter boor about it. Bridge—even for blood—should be viewed as pleasant social relaxation. Don't attempt to rattle an opponent after he has made an unbid slam with a snide comment such as, "Well, we can't bid 'em for you." He may remember the remark and bid like a wild man next time he is your partner. Your only comments when opponents pull a "boo-boo" should be in the nature of sympathetic understanding—addressed to the blameless member of the unfortunate partnership.

Post-mortems help not the deceased.

A detailed dissection of what might have been on any particular hand is usually a terrible waste of time. It rarely teaches your partner anything, and if the post-mortem points the finger of blame squarely at you, you may boot the next hand out of sheer guilt or self-doubt. The best way to shut off this feckless kind of speculation is to claim a total blank as to your holding. And if your partner or an opponent tries to reconstruct it, mutter something subtle, like "Dammit, that was *that* hand. Deal!" If you happen to be dealer, it's embarrasssing but not fatal.

It doesn't pay to pour good money after bad.

Most duplicate players consider each hand in a theoretical vacuum. Money bridge players know better. Pure odds don't do you a whit of good if they lead to a calculated sacrifice of 500 points when you have already spent 500 points on a lost cause. Keep a running balance sheet in your skull. Five hundred points isn't a bad price to pay *once* to prevent a vulnerable game. Paying it three times in a row is mathematical folly.

Know the opposition.

Against good players, play as if you were risking the children's milk money. Take this book to heart chapter and verse and you will win in the long run.

Against poor players or weak-kneed ones, loosen up a little. You can afford a few dubious business doubles, because nine times out of ten your double will panic them into looking for gremlins in distribution, and they will boot the hand.

Given the choice between a takeout double and an overcall, go for the double. It will often terrify the timid into a contract short of an ice-cold game or slam.

With an edge in bidding and playing skill, try for a "set" game at rubber bridge. Even though the stakes are higher at Chicago, you'll win more at rubber bridge, because it gives weak players more opportunity to go wrong. They're much more likely to overbid and underbid, ignore the score, prolong the rubber way past the point where it can possibly pay, and commit other forms of hari-kari once losing psychology sets in.

This devious baker's dozen of pragmatic pointers may make the game seem somehow cold and calculating, but they should not. Bridge, even for blood, should still be fun. Naturally, it is more fun to win than to lose. But bear in mind that contract bridge was originated by a gentleman, and, win or lose, it never pays to be anything but a gentleman.

On this note I reluctantly take my leave of you. Good luck. But if you've read this book carefully, you won't need it.